TO BANG OR NOT TO BANG?
A BOOK OF QUESTIONS

Questions for any gang members who are interested in improving the quality of their lives

Jeorald Pitts a.k.a Lil Tone Tone

A former member of a notorious crip gang has a PH.D in gang experience and a Masters Degree in change from the University of Hard Knocks...

Edited By: Shemeka E. Smith

Published by **Level 4 Publishing (level4publishing@yahoo.com)**
in conjunction with

Trafford PUBLISHING

Order this book online at www.trafford.com
or email orders@trafford.com or tobangornottobang.com

Most Trafford titles are also available at major online book retailers.

© Copyright 2010 Jeorald Pitts, a.k.a Lil Tone Tone.
All rights reserved. No part of this publication may be reproduced, stored in a retrieval system, or transmitted, in any form or by any means, electronic, mechanical, photocopying, recording, or otherwise, without the written prior permission of the author.

Printed in the United States of America.

ISBN: 978-1-4269-3465-0 (soft)
ISBN: 978-1-4269-3566-4 (ebook)

Trafford rev. 7/7/2010

www.trafford.com
North America & international
toll-free: 1 888 232 4444 (USA & Canada)
phone: 250 383 6864 ♦ fax: 812 355 4082

"*TO BANG or NOT TO BANG* questions, educates, intrigues, and surprises in a way that will grab your attention to the point where you will not be able to put it down until there are no more questions to hold you."

Tyra Torian
Mental Health Therapist for Children

"*TO BANG or NOT TO BANG* is an amazing book for both parents and youth that should be in every school and library across the country."

Ujima Thompson
Educator

"What a good job Jeorald "Lil Tone" Pitts has done. His questions, facts, and story pull together so much of what all gang members need to understand about gang bangin'. I encourage all young ridas to read this book. I rate it "real.""

Kenneth Gilliam a.k.a. Foots
Rollin' 60s

"*TO BANG or NOT TO BANG* is the Holy grail of gang intervention and prevention in the world.

Dr. Malik Spellman
Writer for *L.A. Sentinel* newspaper

"This book demonstrates how asking yourself good questions is a good way of keeping it real with yourself. All gang members should ask themselves these questions no matter their race."

Frank Erik Rodriguez
a.k.a. Boy Blue
V*Norwalk

"Perhaps America's most brilliant writer in regards to gang life, I happen to agree with every noun, verb, semi-colon, and comma that Jeorald has written. From the bottom of my heart - THANK YOU THANK YOU THANK YOU."

Janice Hall
Parent

For information about special discounts for bulk purchases please contact tobangornottobang.com or e-mail jp2bangornot2bang@yahoo.com.

Part of the proceeds from the sales of this book will go to:

C.H.A.N.G.E.S.

(Community Helping Adolescence Needing Guidance, Education & Support) Organization

Contents

1. About The Author 1
2. Questions 17
3. Did You Dream Of Being A "Gang Banger" When You Were A Kid? 19
4. At What Age Is It Too Young To Take An Oath For Life? 22
5. Are You On The Front Line? 24
6. What Does It Take To Be In A Gang? 27
7. Who Are You? 28
8. Do You Feel As Though, Due To Your Circumstances Or Surroundings That You Have No Other Choice But To Bang? 30
9. Have You Noticed That Most Gang Members Are Either On Their Way To Jail, Already In Jail, or Just Getting Out Of Jail? 32
10. Is "Homie Love" Real? 33
11. Does Your Gang Have A Retirement Plan? 35
12. What Is To Be Gained Or Won By Gang Wars? 39
13. What Makes You Cool? 41
14. Do You Practice Delayed Gratification? 43
15. Is Killing A Rival Worth Spending The Rest Of Your Life In Prison? . 47
16. Do You Believe In You? 48
17. Are you Really Paying Attention To Your Surroundings? 52
18. Is There Anything Happening Within Your Gang Now That You Thought Would Never Occur? 54
19. Are You Your Own Worst Enemy? 56
20. R U Conscious? 61
21. If You Died Today, What Legacy Would You Leave Behind? 63
22. What Legacy Would You Like To Leave? 69
23. Quest For Answers 74
24. Afterthoughts 87
25. Letters 92
26. Why? 95

DEDICATIONS

This book is dedicated to my father, Sabra Pitts, and to Dean Hogan (may they both rest in peace), also to all those who have lost their lives to gang violence.

About The Author

In the book of life there have been many eras of gangs, however, the last 3 generations were born into the chapters of notoriously violent street gangs. I entered the pages on March 10, 1971 at General Hospital in Los Angeles, CA. I was brought up in a family of opposites in a lower middle class neighborhood on the southwest side of Los Angeles. My father was an unemotional man, a serious gambler, and business owner. My Momma was a playful and very loving housewife and dedicated Jehovah's Witness. Aside from me, my family's household consisted of my 2 brothers and 3 sisters. Bobby, the oldest, was a loner and decided to be a soldier in the U.S. Navy to protect and serve his country. My other brother, Tony, had a lot of friends and decided to be a soldier in a gang that was destroying communities. As for my sisters, they ranged from light- to chocolate-skinned and all equally pretty; however, that's where there similarities end. My oldest sister, Denise, was short and very spunky. She was an original criplette gang member who enjoyed using drugs and had a negative outlook on life. My other sister, Cherise, was a tall, charming, intelligent, workaholic who never used drugs and had a positive outlook on life. I guess you can say I was a mixture of them all. So was my sister, Crystal, who came along 7 years behind me.

As a kid, I had an overload of energy and interest that always kept me into something - mainly money-making adventures. I was a pretty good kid and rarely got into trouble other than getting caught playing "naked doctor" and "show me yours and I'll show you mine" with the little girls in my neighborhood. I had big dreams of becoming a movie producer and professional baseball player. However, I didn't get to play organized sports much due to me spending my Saturdays at the Kingdom Hall for Jehovah's Witnesses, which were the days that most of the games were played. I also had a dream of owning businesses like my father who told me at a young age that money makes the world go around. I sure was willing to do my part to keep my world spinning, which my father encouraged.

I used to mow lawns, wash cars, make and sell frozen kool-aid icy cups, and candy at the park that we lived right across the street from. I

Jeorald Pitts, a.k.a Lil Tone Tone

even created my own game to make money. I called it "Take a Shot". It was made out of a large pickle jar. I cut a slit in the top just big enough to drop coins through. I placed a small shot glass inside of the jar directly in the middle, then put a bunch of shiny coins along the sides and filled it up with water. If someone dropped a coin and made it into the shot glass, they would win double the amount that landed in the glass. I would take it to the park and kids and adults alike would enjoy playing. It was like a mini slot machine. I was raking in the dough along with my father's praises.

When I was 7 years old, my brother, Tony, was shot twice. Once in the face with a shotgun, which caused him to be totally blind, and also in the side by a 38, which caused him to be temporarily paralyzed on the left side of his body. This event took place while my brother was a mere 14 years of age by rival gang members on his way home from the skating rink. As a direct result of the shooting, he had to spend an entire year in the hospital and was unable to talk. When he **was** finally able to speak, do you know the first thing he said to me? He did not tell me that he loved me. He did not tell me not to ever gangbang. He **did**, however, tell me to bring him his blue rag the next time that I visited him; this would leave a profound image in my young mind. My mother was crushed by my brother getting shot; thus, she would warn me often to stay away from gangbanging. My mother was determined to not allow me to be taken in by the thug life style and make me into a good little Jehovah's Witness. I do not know if it was rebellion or fate, but due to my brother and sister being the highly respected gang members that they both were – along with two of my first cousins who lived across the street from us – I was exposed to their gangbanging homeboys and boyfriends on a daily basis. Even the co-founder of the crips, Stanley "Tookie" Williams (rest in peace) came around trying to date my oldest sister. I was hit in the eyes at a very young age with a deformed image of manhood and coolness that was already starting to blind me.

I had my father's business sense and zest for the finer things in life, but my universe revolved around my mother. I guess this is my way of saying that I was a momma's boy. I loved my mother and really wanted to please her. Yet it seemed that the more that I tried to please her and Jehovah with being a good little Christian boy and following all of their strict rules, the more I would end up rebelling against them out of my mother's presence. You can best believe though, that **in** her presence, I was the perfect Jehovah's Witness son that she wanted.

To Bang or Not To Bang: A Book of Questions

I remember a time in particular when I was around 9 or 10 years old and my mom and I were out in field service knocking on doors early in the morning – which I am sure most of you are familiar with. On this particular day, we went to this one house and I was giving my speech and offering the lady of the house the latest Watch Tower and Awake magazines when her son came to the door. He looked me dead in my face and said "Momma, that's the boy who beat me up after school because I told him what you told me, that gangs are for cowards. He is not a real Jehovah's Witness. He is a Neighborhood Crip." My mother did not believe this at first, but the boy just kept going on and on and then he started crying. I was so surprised that I was not even able to put on a good defense. My mother's high-yellow face turned bright red with anger. Needless to say that I got my butt whipped and had to wear 3-piece suits and dress shoes to school for the remainder of the school year among other punishments. I would live this double life of good Jehovah Witness and wanna-be gang member until I was 12 years old.

When I reached junior high school my brother's (Tony) name was legendary and was still being whispered throughout school hallways. At times, the teachers and counselors would tell students about his gangbanging and being shot and blinded all while a student at the school with the hopes of trying to discourage gang bangers. But since my brother was still actively banging **and** totally blind, the complete opposite happened. It only added to his legend at the school. When I arrived, it seemed that everybody expected me to be as down as my brother. This pressure I felt was heavy, but I decided to not only live up to his reputation, but to try and surpass it.

Even with me being a gangbanger, at the age of 13, I was very mature and business savvy. I was running my father's arcade business – which was equipped with 20 video games, multiple pool tables, and stocked with refreshments for sale – all by myself. I opened the store up after school and closed it at 11:00 at night when my father would pick me up. The only problem was that the arcade was located in a rival turf. Due to the respect my father had and the fact that I wasn't over there gangbanging or disrespecting them, they allowed me to work there. This was the case until one day I got into a fight with one of the rival gang members. He felt that I should not be allowed on their turf. He would later come back and shoot up the arcade with me inside, making it unsafe for us to do business; so my father had to close the arcade down due to my gang affiliation – causing him to lose out on a lot of money. My father was really upset but he was not the lecturing type. He would instead ask me questions that would

Jeorald Pitts, a.k.a Lil Tone Tone

stay on my mind much longer than a lecture. This time he asked me **"Do you love your gang more than you love me?"** I answered "No I don't". He then asked, "Well why are you letting your gang activities take money out of my pockets?"

My dad did not know what to do to about my gangbanging. He tried putting me to work – but it did not work out. He would also give me a Cadillac Seville when I was in the 8th grade as a tool to try to get me to behave and not bang. The car came with rules, such as, do not miss school, do not drive beyond a certain area, and do not be involved in any gang activity. I was really excited about having the car and even more excited that it was a Cadillac. I know that I was fortunate. I had always done well in the competitive games that teenage boys played for the attention of girls. So you can just imagine that having a Cadillac really put the odds in my favor. Now you know that I was *really* trying to follow the rules. Then, one day one of my homeboys had gotten jumped on at another school by rival gang members. He, along with two of my other homeboys, ran up to my car and told me what happened with looks of payback and revenge on their faces. I caved under the peer pressure and told them to "get in and let's roll". We went up to the school and spotted them (the rivals) walking down the street. I pulled up and we all jumped out right in the middle of the street and clashed with them. The car was sitting in the middle of the street with the doors flung wide open, stopping traffic. My father just so happened to be passing by and saw us fighting. But before he could even turn around in traffic and get back to the scene, we were gone. Later that same day when he came home he took the car from me. He would also punish me with a new tool of discipline – a pool stick cut in half with an Oakley bicycle grip on the end. He was punishing me not only for the incident of earlier today, but also because this was the same day that he found out that I had taken on my brother's gang name – Lil Tone Tone. My choice to walk in the footsteps of someone who, after being shot and blinded due to gang banging, did not learn anything, was *still* banging totally blind, and was currently in prison instead of walking in his footsteps – a man who was a pretty successful businessman (owning several businesses), providing for his family, and owning a nice home with a Mercedes Benz pretty much sent my dad over the edge. He also had a dream of running his businesses with his son, me; which I was ruining. The thrashing that I took would have taken the "gang" *and* the "bang" out of most gangbangers. I had oow whee knots from the bottom of my feet to the top of my head. My father decided to drop a few of his famous questions on me before he left the room. He asked, *"Did you know that your mom and I almost moved into the same neighborhood that the boys you were fighting are from instead of the neighborhood you're from? If we would have moved to that area, what gang do you think you would have been from then?"* He would never discipline me with that pool stick again. I think he was afraid of really hurting me. But as soon as all of the knots went down I turned my banging up. My name was starting to become the talk of the neighborhood. However, since my father was always working, he was rarely aware of my activities.

My sister Cherise, however, heard about some of my gang stunts and tried talking to me; but I was too stupid to listen. I was running down the dead-end street of jail or death so fast that my sister thought it would be safer for me to be a drug dealer than a gangbanger. She had her boyfriend, who was a big-time drug dealer, try to talk to me. One day after school, he showed up in his new fly Benz and picked me up. We went to a fancy restaurant and over our meal he told me that my sister was really concerned about me getting hurt. He wanted to take me out of town with him where I could make a lot of money. He then looked me in the eyes with a deadly look and said "But you will have to leave that gangbanging nonsense alone because you can't bang and make money at the same time". Afterwards, he asked me, *"Do you want to bang or ball like me?"* without even questioning myself, I looked him directly in his eyes and said "I want to bang!"

He appeared very puzzled by my answer. I could not tell whether there was disappointment in his eyes or anger, but there was definitely surprise. I imagine that due to the opportunity he felt he was offering to me and my turning it down, he would later tell my sister that I was too banged out! Yeah, just like many of you, I was in love with my hood and living on the edge. I craved the excitement of defying death motivated by youthful energy, impatience, and a rebellious spirit. I too had little or no interest in education or doing the right thing. I was just rushing forward into the world ill-prepared for life's critical choices that continued to overwhelm me.

However, I did have moments when I displayed who Jeorald was instead of Lil Tone Tone. I recall one day arriving at school to find out that one of the few fellow 9th graders at our school who did not gangbang was shot and killed. I was saddened by the news and on the spot, I started going around collecting money for his family from all of the kids at school. I collected over $500.00 in one day; with me making the biggest donation, my lunch money for the week. I told all those who donated that I would be ditching school the next day to go purchase his family something nice from all of us and that they were welcome to come with me. The next day, about 65 students met up with me and we went to the local mall. We purchased a plaque in his memory, some flowers, and big cards. We all signed the cards and left a personal message or our fondest memories of our fallen classmate. We caught the bus to his mother's house. I will never forget the expression on her face when I rang the bell and she answered the door to a sea of youth covering her whole front lawn. I told her who we were and why we were there. I presented her with the plaque, flowers, cards, and the remainder of the money that I had collected.

Tears started rolling down her face. They appeared to be in slow motion and seemed to wet all of us at the same time, because we all started crying. Yet her tears were not so much the tears of sorrow. She had a big smile on her face. The fact that her son had so many school mates that cared made her feel good even if it was only for that brief moment. This happened many years ago; but as I write this, the memory is still so vivid to me, it seems like it happened just yesterday.

Even though I was a gangbanger, some of my mom's morals and her religious values were instilled in me. I liked good more than evil. I enjoyed speaking the truth more than lying. I have always respected my elders and others. The only people who got problems from me were rival gang members.

The following day at school I was called to the Principal's office. I was in trouble for collecting money on school grounds, ditching, and encouraging others to ditch. The Principal, a no-nonsense type, respected what I had done and only gave me a firm warning to not do it again and a few days in detention.

Not long afterwards, on my way to school, I was rack packed and beaten up pretty badly by eight rival gang members. I came right back and took revenge against those involved. Due to these actions, I would be arrested for the first time and sent to the California Youth Authority for assault with a deadly weapon.

Upon my release, after 2½ years, I really wanted to change and function as a man in society instead of as a member of a gang. My father was doubtful of my desire to really change; but still, he showed his faith in me. He gave me a tow truck that needed a motor and a work truck that had a candy-apple paint on it. He told me with a fatherly look on his face, "Son you can make money with both of these vehicles that I'm giving you". But since my father always had to end all of his talks with a question, he asked, **"Why am I giving you a tow truck that needs a motor?"** I responded, "Because you want me to prove that I really want it by **getting** a new motor". He smiled and said, "Right on!"

I got a job working construction for 10 hours a day doing hard labor. I moved in with my girlfriend, who had her own house.

I was living paycheck to paycheck with having to do the "grown man thing". Paying house bills and making payments on a new motor for my tow truck. One morning on my way to work I stopped by my parents' house to borrow some money for lunch. Upon leaving their house, I noticed that I had a flat tire and my spare tire was also flat. I sat there on the curb right in front of the rear left tire in the rain thinking, *what am I going to do?* I did not have enough money to buy a tire and I did not want to borrow any more money from my parents – whom I was already in debt to – beyond the amount of my paycheck. As I was still sitting there, my homeboy, K.K., who was in the youth authority with me and had recently been released, rolled up. He saw my truck and pulled up in his new Cadillac on Dayton rims and Vogue tires (Daytons back then were like what 24" rims are now-a-days). Thinking that I was inside because he couldn't see me behind my truck, he turned his music up figuring that I would hear it and come outside. But I just sat there in a daze and did not move. I can still hear the swishing sound in my head because of the way his new Vogue tires sounded against the rain water as he pulled away. The rain seemed like it was dropping on my head to the beat of his loud music. At that moment I thought, *here it is that I'm working hard every day, but don't have any money to buy a tire and I've been out four month; but my homie, who had only been out for one month and selling drugs, has a new Cadillac on expensive rims.*

I sat there in the rain for over an hour wrestling with right and wrong. The conclusion I came to would change the course of my life for the worse. I decided to quit my job and start selling drugs. This decision caused me to hang out in my neighborhood more and eventually I would be sucked right back into front-line banging.

In the beginning I was doing pretty well with my hustling. I bought a brand new Astro Van and even got a motor for my tow truck. I started two small businesses – a towing service and a lawn service – trying to do the right things plus slang and bang.

My gang was at constant war with everyone at this time. One afternoon I was coming back from a funeral for one of my homeboy's who had gotten

Jeorald Pitts, a.k.a Lil Tone Tone

gunned down a week earlier while I was on my way to the hospital to visit another one who had gotten shot in the mouth the night before. I was at a stop light when some rivals pulled up next to me and started shooting. I didn't even notice them until the shooting started. I pressed on the gas while bullets were assaulting me and my van. The glass from the windows fell down on me like hail from a storm. I was shot in my back and hand, which caused me to lose control and run a red light crashing into a car and flipping my van over. After all of this I ended up losing my lawn service clients while recuperating from my wounds. I was forced to sale my tow truck to pay to get my van fixed – this was due to the van being in my father's name and if I didn't, it would have affected his credit.

I found myself hanging a lot more with my homeboy, Baby Weasel. He was a little guy with a big heart and very generous with his time and bullets for our enemies, but showed little interest in hustling. If he was your friend, he was your best friend. If he was your enemy, he was your worst enemy.

After getting shot, almost totaling my Astro van, and losing my tow truck and lawn services, I started going to different states selling drugs – trying to come back up. I quickly began to make lots of money. I started slowing way down on my banging, but the more my money grew, the more my reputation grew, and the more my enemies grew. My name was coming up in incidents and shootings that I had nothing to do with. Even Baby Weasel had stopped being so sharing with his bullets and started to show interest in making some money.

My mom would always say, "If you're not doing things the right way something always goes wrong."Low and behold - my homeboy, who was a heavy-set, soft-spoken go-getter named Pete; and myself were rumored to have murdered someone.

A contract was quickly placed on our lives. It was not long before there was an unsuccessful attempt on my life that left me luckily unharmed. Pete, however, did not fare too well as he was ambushed outside of his house and shot in the face at point-blank range. He would survive the attack, but with one less eye. We were being hunted by unknown enemies. It was as if everyone wanted to cash in on our deaths.

One month later, Pete, Baby Weasel, and I were getting into our cars in the parking lot of a strip club, when once again someone tried to cash in on the contracts. We were ambushed in broad daylight by a man with a machine gun.

To Bang or Not To Bang: A Book of Questions

After a shootout, I was shot in the arm; Pete was shot eight times, but survived once again; however, unfortunately, Baby Weasel, who was only shot one time in the side, would not be so lucky. His death really affected me. My heart and mind were broken into pieces. I thought the only thing that would glue them back together was revenge. A few days later, the 1992 Rebellion Riots broke out and soon after I would be arrested and charged for the rumored murder. All of the money, toys, low riders, motorcycle, and cars that I had gotten from putting my life on the line while selling drugs all now had to go towards paying attorneys. After a flawed trial, I would be convicted.

At sentencing, I did not have a chance to duck when the judge through the book at me and hit me with a 30 year- to life-sentence at the age of 21. It was not just one event, but a series of bad choices that left me standing in that courtroom dazed.

Innocent of the crime or guilty by law, I consider myself one of the lucky ones to have received a life sentence and a chance to change my self-destructive ways; as opposed to many of my homeboys and other unfortunate gang members who received a death sentence by the streets - a sentence I am sure was awaiting me. Even my homeboy K.K. would be eventually taken by the streets. I am not trying to impress you with any of the stories from my violent past. In fact, I have left many of the more violent ones out. However, I *am* trying to impress **upon** you just how much I have changed. For the past 12 years, I have fought and thoroughly studied gangs' addictive allure – which had me handcuffed to my gang for over 20 years – coming up with strategies, answers, and key questions that would help me free myself. I did this while in a small world ruled by gangs – a California Level 4 maximum prison. Here is where some gang members have lost their lives in attempts to leave their gangs; a place I had only seen two ways that high-ranking gang members could successfully leave their gangs with little problems, turning their lives over to God or Allah, or going into protective custody. I would not choose either of these options, for my heart revolted against them. I did not feel like I needed God, Allah, or the prison's protection to do what I knew I had to do in order to become a man for the first time at the age of 31. I have now been a man and free from the gang life for the past 8 years and I will share with you how throughout this book.

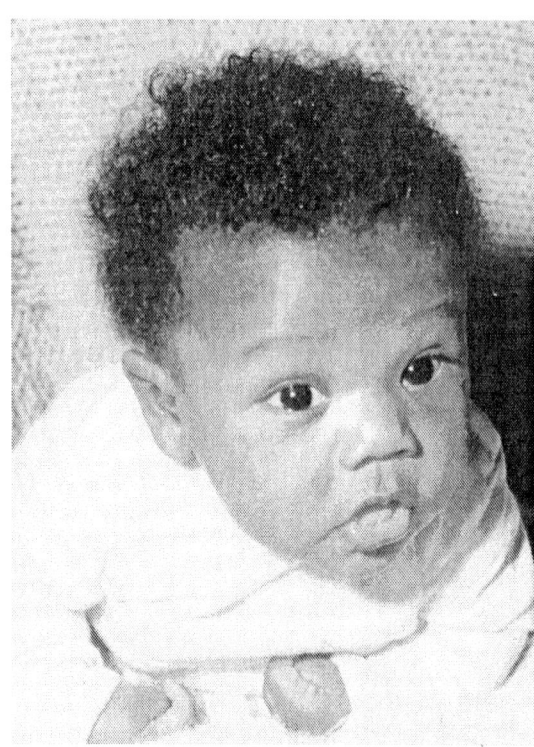

Jeorald at 6 months.

Jeorald at age 10 with his sister Crystal.

Jeorald and his family posing for a picture right after his 6th grade graduation.

Jeorald's parents, Sabra and Cathy Pitts, in Las Vegas (1986)

Lil Tone in the 8th grade.

K*K, Lil Donut, Crazy Toons, and Lil Tone, mid '80s at Henry Clay Junior High

*Lil Tone and Baby Weasel
(R.I.P), in 1990*

*Lil Tone and Baby Weasel
(R.I.P) hangin' out*

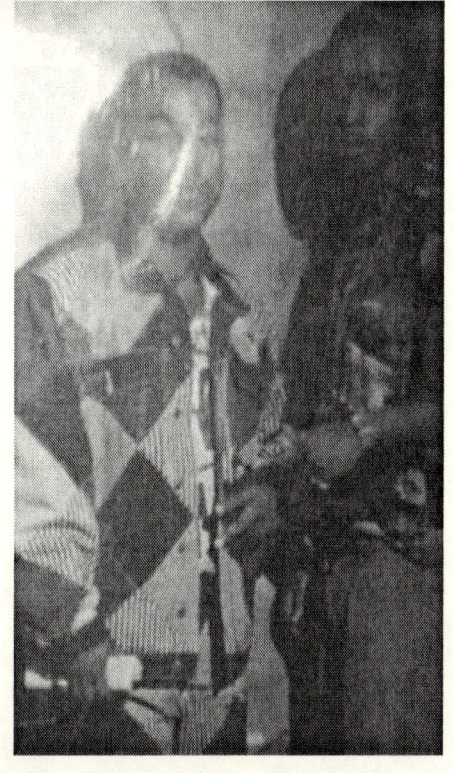

Lil Tone on his way to a Dub-C concert.

Lil Tone poses for a picture in a club in 1991.

Lil Tone and Ant (R.I.P) at a pajama party (1992).

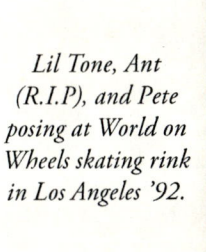

Lil Tone, Ant (R.I.P), and Pete posing at World on Wheels skating rink in Los Angeles '92.

Lil Tone on his 21st Birthday

Lil Tone and Ant (R.I.P) in 1992.

Questions

The dictionary defines the word "question" as a verb, (1) to ask questions; (2) doubt, dispute; (3) subject to analysis; (4) examine, quiz.

Yet questions are much more than the definitions found in the dictionary. In fact, there would be no need for a dictionary without questions because the dictionary is a book of answers to questions of spelling and definitions and so on. Thinking itself is nothing but the system of asking and answering questions. Think about it.

In the following pages you will be asked questions that you might have to ask yourself a few times to pull down the answers that reside within you. The key is you have to ask yourself these questions with the confidence of getting an answer. But do not blindly accept anything I say or anyone else. Make sure you question it to see if it makes sense to you.

Some of the questions in this book were born in my mind, but many of them were posed to me over the years by my now-deceased father (may he rest in peace) in his many attempts to get me to open my mind and really think about my gang life style. However, it took a sentence of 30 to life, plus many other setbacks and trips to the hole for me to finally find my answers to these questions that would change me from a mindless gang member to a man mindful of the destruction that gangbanging causes. Hopefully it will not be so costly for you to find your answers.

I will pose some of these same questions to you and give you some information that may assist you in finding your own answers. The right answers cannot be given to you, you must find them within yourself; but you *can* be given the right questions. I have learned that a person can only gain understanding of themselves when they ask themselves insightful questions, not when they are spoon-fed someone elses answers. Asking yourself insightful questions is a way of keeping it real with yourself.

Most gang bangers think they know it all so they never bother to question themselves or their actions. These questions you are about to read in the following chapters can be empowering if you use them to really examine the soundness of the beliefs that you may have just blindly accepted in the past. Many of our beliefs are supported by information

Jeorald Pitts, a.k.a Lil Tone Tone

we have received from others that we failed to question at the time. If you take a look at them now, you may find that what you have unconsciously believed for years may be based on a false set of principles or ideas. As you ask yourself these questions, some, which may cause you to feel mad, sad, enlightened, or regretful; there may be a trial in your heart. Let your conscious be your judge.

Did You Dream Of Being A "Gang Banger" When You Were A Kid?

It is difficult for me to imagine that many kids growing up say either of the following: "When I get older I want to gang bang", "I want to get shot", or "I want to go to the pen (penitentiary, prison) and do hard time".

What were your dreams before you started bangin'? I know you grew up in a neighborhood where it was probably easier to get a gun than a library card, in a place where there was more opportunity to join a gang than join a little league team, or a place where your school yards may have been more violent than prison yards.

However, it does not make your dreams any less valued or meaningless, because of the area you were raised in.

Some people choose to use poverty and low social class as an excuse to give up on their dream and take the easy way out. They choose to become part of the negativity that stole their dream in the first place.

Do you still think it is possible to achieve your dreams? If your answer is yes, then **why are you allowing the realities of your hood to hold your dreams hostage?** If your answer is no, I will not burden you with all of the facts and statistics regarding all of the people who, despite once being in gangs, or growing up in bad communities, are going after their goals an achieving their dreams. I'll leave that to those more educated than I.

I *will* tell you about a few I know about. Roc grew up in an unruly turf. The Projects is where he was raised on a steady diet of violence from a very early age. Therefore, it was no surprise that at the age of 13, he was in reform school. By the age of 17, he was convicted of manslaughter – for taking another life in a knife fight.

While out on parole he was busted with a pistol and was sent back to prison. When a riot broke out in the prison, he was sent to the "hole" for socking a guard. During this time in the "hole", he began reading books.

Jeorald Pitts, a.k.a Lil Tone Tone

What happened next is a great story of growth. When he was released from the "hole", he had a new outlook on life and new dreams. He began studying for his G.E.D., and created a prison drama program.

Upon his release, he went to college and changed his life.

Do you know who Roc Is? His true name is Charles S. Dutton. He is an actor. You may have seen him in his old T.V. series "Roc". You may have also seen him in such movies as "Rudy", "A Time to Kill", and/or many others. He also appeared on Broadway, for which he was nominated for two "Tony Awards".

The second story is a personal story. It is about one of my childhood homeboys.

We came up in a savage, gang-infested neighborhood. We both joined the gang at young ages.

The junior high school we attended was one of the worst in the Los Angeles School District.

Reg and I would patrol the hallways looking for trouble. In school and in the neighborhood, there existed an entire power structure based on who could kick whose ass. It was a street version of "King of the Hill". After school plans for fights and "bum rushes", often with weapons, were drawn up and promoted with "Strike Force-" and "Don King-" like skills.

The school bell had dual meanings. It meant the end of the school day for some, but for Reg, I, and others, the sound meant "let's get ready to rumble!"

After school brawling for the gangs was like an unofficial "b-team" and varsity sport. Reg was always involved in the action.

After junior high, and shortly after entering high school, Reg stopped buying into the idea that banging was the way. He began to slowly cut back on hanging out and banging. He began placing that energy into sports and his education.

He took his childhood dreams from his mental shelf and began to clean the dust off. He graduated from high school then went on to college, where he achieved one of his dreams – getting his PhD in education. This is one of the highest academic degrees.

Now, he walks the same school hallways that he once terrorized as Doctor Reggie Sample, Vice Principal.

There are many more stories like these. Your dreams do not have an expiration date unless you give them one. Your dreams are still in your hands, you just have to grab on to this profound reality.

I know you have dreams that still play out in the theater of your mind that with time and energy, you can play out on the big stage of life.

What do you have to lose by giving the time and energy to your dreams that just may help you achieve them? You must realize that success is a choice - your choice to get what you want. However, it helps to know what you want, so dream on.

At What Age Is It Too Young To Take An Oath For Life?

(A TRUE STORY ABOUT MY WIFE)

When I met her, I was in elementary school. She was older than me, and I was claiming her as my girlfriend before I actually knew what a girlfriend was. I knew just because I was hanging with her that people thought I was "hard" and "cool".

She was born and raised in my neighborhood. Her parents let her run wild, so she was very mature and street savvy for her age. She was attractive to both young and old. When I was 13 years old, she asked me to marry her and I gladly accepted in a ceremony that made her my wife for life. I was madly in love with her and she had me growing up fast. I was doing grown-up things like getting high and drinking. We were having a lot of fun in the beginning – going to picnics, concerts, and doing a lot of dirt together. We were like "Bonnie & Clyde". She was very demanding of my time and she wanted me to be with her 24/7. She was very jealous when I tried to do anything that was not centered around her. She would always whisper sweet nothings in my ear and tell me how tuff I was. She would also tell me how I could be the baddest dude in L.A. if I stuck by her. It felt good to have a wife I could call mine.

I got three tattoos; all representing her, so everyone would know that she was my wife.

As I began to get older and mature, I noticed signs that my wife was not capable of showing me the kind of love and dedication that I had shown her. But, I made an oath an as they say, "love is blind" and I was in love, for real.

I felt as though I had the baddest wife in L.A. but due to her aggressive nature, I was always into something – "taking off on fools" or "getting jumped". I've been shot two different times and I've shot people while defending her honor. Some of my homeboys have lost their lives due to some of the madness that she had us into. However, my wife always had our backs when it came to violence.

After being married for only a couple of years, she encouraged me to shoot one of her enemies. When I did it, I was arrested and sent to the California Youth Authority (CYA) for two and a half years.

She didn't **even** stay down for me. She wrote once in a while and sent money every "blue moon". She never came to visit, yet I was still running around bragging and showing everyone my pictures so that they could see how my wife was out there doing it.

I had to rely on my family to take care of me. My family tried hard to tell me, and to get me to see that my wife was a very bad influence on me; but, I was too "sprung" to see it.

As soon as I was released I kicked it with my family for a few hours. Then I was back on the block with my wife. Yeah, I ran straight back to her. She was the only woman that I ever loved. I was trying to kick it and stay out of trouble, but my wife always had something crackin'. It was not too long before I was back in the mix of things. Things were good for a while, then, one day everything went all bad. Once again, I had to let cats know that they could not mess with my wife. It was because of this that I am stuck in the pen doing life. My wife barely writes, she never comes to visit me, nor does she give me any money towards my appeal attorney. I'm in here for loving and being loyal to her, while she is out there doing her own thing. Meanwhile, I am still in here representing her, tattoos and all. I would tell anyone who asks how much I love my wife, no matter what.

Am I crazy in love, or what? We have over twenty years together and I can say that I have been loyal and dedicated through all the pain and suffering.

I went through all of this because of the vow and oath that I made to her when I was a kid. Not mature enough to understand what I was doing, I did not have any idea that things would turn out the way they did. ***Do you think I'm a fool?***

Would you get a divorce from a one-sided situation where you are the only one always suffering just because at a young age you took an oath for life? I am sure most of you would get a divorce!

I am happy to report that I finally got the willpower to divorce my wife, after all these years of marriage, 8 years ago.

The wife that I'm speaking of in this story is none other than my gang...

All gang bangers are married to their gang. ***How much suffering will you take due to an oath you made at such a young age?***

Are You On The Front Line?

A frontline gang member by definition is one who is actively turned up, hangin' and bangin' daily; the key word being "actively".

I ask you, **how many front line gang bangers are really rich or successful?** The answer should help you realize that the gang banging lifestyle does not lead to riches or success. If your answer is "Dub-C", "Snoop Dogg", "The Game", or any other high-profile rapper, understand that they are former gang members or they represent their turf. They are not front line active. If they actually did half of the things they talk about on their records, they would be locked up with me.

There are hundreds of thousands of gang members in the U.S. **Can you name one, who is a turned-up frontline banger, who is putting in work for their hood and really papered up?**

You may see a few of your dope-dealing or "jacker" homies riding in the fly cars on big rims and with their chromed-out Harleys. Trust that they are only one mistake away from being in jail and losing all of their toys in order to pay for their attorney fees. Do not be fooled, even these gang members who are having a little money had to step back from the frontline to get it.

Bangin' and money do not mix. Gang banging retards success. You do not have to believe me, look around. **How many bangers are really rich?** Education and money go hand in hand. The only thing you are going to get by being on the frontline is to be in front of everybody else to go to jail or get shot or killed.

The only place riches and gangbanging come together is in a gang banger's mind, no place else.

*WHAT DO YOU VALUE
MOST IN LIFE?*

What Does It Take To Be In A Gang?

If gangs had a marketing and advertising campaign designed to get people to join, their billboards would read something like this: "Gang Members Wanted. Must Be Tough. No Education or Brains Required. All Ages and Gender's Accepted".

Almost anyone can join a gang. You do not have to have any form of education, brains, or special skills as long as you are "down" or "tough". If gangs had an educational requirement to become a member - for example: say you had to have a 7th grade level of Social Studies, Math, and Reading skills – *how many of your homies would not meet these simple requirements?*

Gangs are recruiting machines, and the more members that they have, the more powerful they feel. As long as you have an appetite for violence, you can join a gang. You may even rise up to become highly respected while never learning to read and/or write. *Why is it that you get jumped into a gang, yet, no test is required?* Your level of intelligence has to be tested in order to join any of the armed forces – ARMY, NAVY, MARINES, or the AIRFORCE. You even have to be tested to go into the next grade level in school, but gangs do not want to test your level of intelligence. They only want to test your level of violence or loyalty to the gang; in fact, the crazier you are, the more respect you will have among the gang.

Just look at some of the words used to describe your most respected homeboys or homegirls – down, crazy, loco, a fool, a nut, loced-out, retarded, turned-up, and/or ignorant. Think about this. *Have you ever heard of a gang member being highly respected within his gang for being smart, getting good grades, scoring high on their SAT's, not missing a day of school, or for getting into a good college?*

How can you be so proud of being a part of something where the crazy and loced-out are highly respected or looked up to, but the smart and educated are looked down at' especially when it is a well-known fact that knowledge is power and the key to success?

Who Are You?

A gang member's identity consists of the decisions they make about who they are and what roles they have decided to connect themselves to. Within this life, they have become the labels they have given themselves.

Most gang bangers take pieces of other gang members' character and style, whom they have looked up to and added to their own identity – riders, shooters, hustler and leader coolness, their way of dressing, and so on. Your ideas about who you are, creates the limits within which you live and what you will or will not do. To put it simply, what you do is who you are.

A majority of gang members are so linked to their gangs that they mistakenly believe that they are no one apart from their gang. *Have you ever noticed when someone asks a gang banger his/her name, he has to tell them where he/she is from as well? Who are you, really? Are you more than just a gang member?* The best way you can get to know yourself is to question yourself. *Are you a son, a daughter, uncle, aunt, brother, or sister? Are you rude, respectful, honest or dishonest? Are you positive or negative, shy or outgoing? Are you orderly or messy, caring or uncaring? Are you bright or not so bright, down beat or upbeat?* All of these things and more are a part of who you are. Your identity does not just lie in you being a gang banger.

Do you like the person you are? Many bangers do not believe that they have it in themselves to be who they are capable of being; therefore, they try to make themselves content with being less than who they are, and they try to be good at being bad.

If you could change anything, what would you change about yourself? I know some of you have desires to expand or redefine who you are, but the uncertainty that comes along with this new identity scares you; so you stay stuck in your role as a banger. Many people have fears of uncertainty or of the unknown – fear of taking on something new or a new role in life. Many would rather take on the grief that their roles offer that they are familiar with, rather than to take on fear of the unknown. I am sure some of you, as I did, had a fear of the unknown when you first took on the identity or role of a gang banger. But you dealt with it, just as you can now. Your actions got you into banging, and your actions will get you out.

Gang banging is not ***who*** you are, it is simply ***what*** you do. Thus, you can give up that role and take on a new one without giving up yourself. The good thing about this is that you can choose pieces from people who are living the lifestyle you want to live. Then, you can build a new identity as a man or woman, not as a member, and live up to it as well; because who you are is largely believing who you can be.

Who are you?

Do You Feel As Though, Due To Your Circumstances Or Surroundings That You Have No Other Choice But To Bang?

If the answer to your question is yes, is it because of your circumstances, surroundings, or yourself? In any case you ***do*** have a choice. Despite your starting point or your current situation, anything is possible. I know the only reality you see is the one you are choosing to live every day; but there are realities that you are not allowing yourself to see. I agree that you may not be able to choose your current circumstances, but you can choose your thoughts and actions, which will one day create your future circumstances.

In my youth, my blindness in regards to banging would not allow me to see myself as anything other than a banger. I suppose this is why I am locked up now.

Each of us possesses a spark of talent that, with dedication and practice, we are capable of doing something special in our lives; which can lead us in the direction of a rewarding and thrilling career. Even if you cannot see your talents, they are there. Some people take longer to see their talents than others. You may have the athletic talents of "Kobe Bryant", the boxing talents of "Oscar De La Hoya", the business talent of "Russell Simmons", the humor of "George Lopez", the mental talents of "Barrack Obama", the rapping talents of "Lil Wayne", the singing talent of "Baby Bash", and/or the acting talent of "Denzel Washington".

Each person must discover their talents in life and either they will develop them or they will betray them. If you do not tap into your talent, at best, you will become a small image of the person you could be. I know you have a special talent storming inside of you just waiting on you to give it the chance to rain down on the world. ***Will you discover and develop the talents you have or will you betray them?***

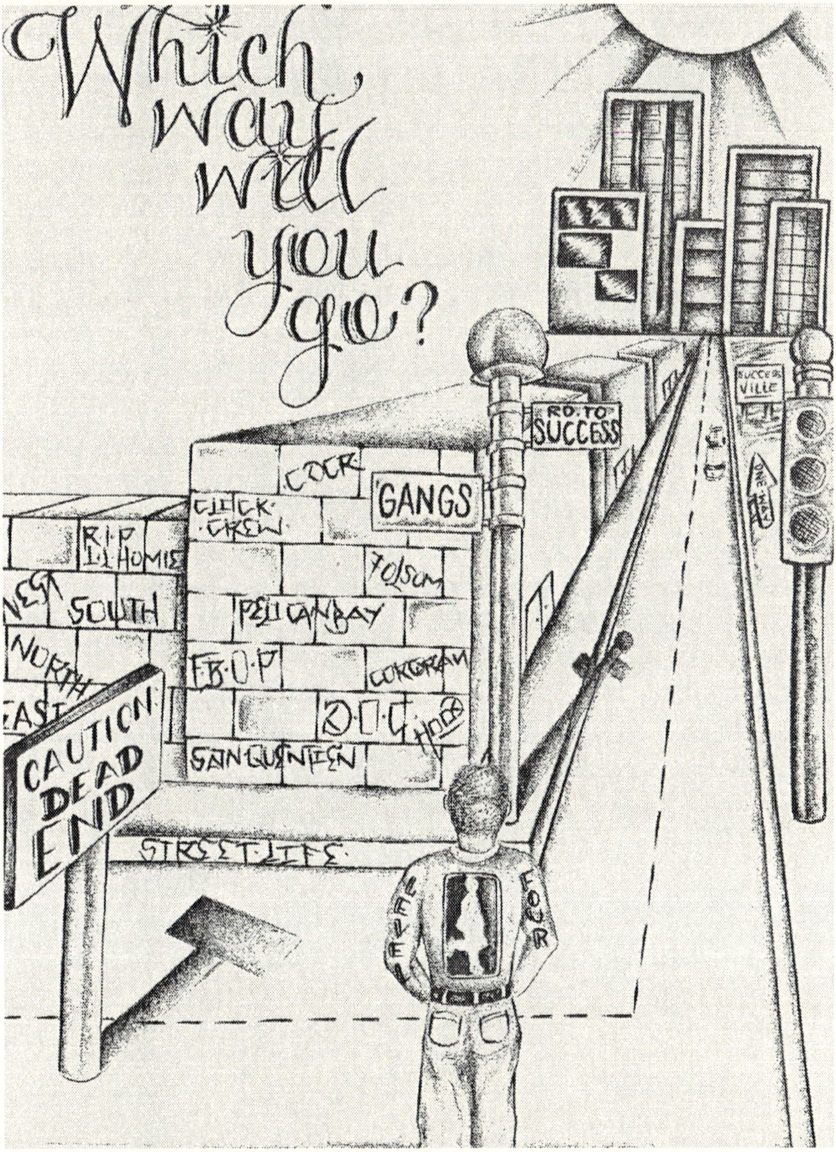
Which way will you go?
RD. TO SUCCESS
GANGS
SOUTH
NORTH
EAST
PELICAN BAY
CORCORAN
CAUTION DEAD END
STREET LIFE
FOUR

Have You Noticed That Most Gang Members Are Either On Their Way To Jail, Already In Jail, or Just Getting Out Of Jail?

Street gangs have designed their styles from certain elements of prison – their saggy and baggy pants, their big shirts, bald heads, and even the poses they use when taking pictures all come from prison. So, it is not surprising for gang members to think that they will one day go to jail or prison since their styles glorify it.

Jail is where most gang members believe that their manhood is best tested and developed; so it will not take much imagination for one of them to think of jail as a second home or even a first home. Jail serves as a home for so many gang members. It is where they get three meals a day, a place to sleep - luxuries that some of them cannot even get in free society – where you have to have money to buy food or starve, find shelter or be homeless. Do not get caught up in the revolving jail door.

Ask yourself, "*What do I have to do to stay out of jail?*" The answers that will help you stay free are within you. *Jail and prison are for people who cannot make it in society. Can you?*

Is "Homie Love" Real?

Can you give someone something that you do not have? To have real love for someone, first you have to "really" love yourself. Most people agree that when someone really loves themselves, they try to put themselves in the best position possible to do well and have good things happen for them, and to stay out of harm's way.

It is a well-known fact that gang members do time in jail sooner or later, which is definitely *not* the best position to be in. They end up with felonies on their records, disqualifying them from most of the good-paying jobs – which would not be putting themselves in a positive position to do well. They often put themselves in harm's way because gang members are always at high-risk of getting shot at, shot up, and/or killed. So, by definition, gang members have no real love for themselves. A gang's basic principles ensure that you will not really love yourself; because if you **did** love yourself, it would be much harder for you to harm someone who looks like you. It would make it much more difficult for you to put your life on the line without a purpose or a cause for your gang. This is why gangs do not encourage racial pride or education of self upon its members. Doing so brings about self love. *So, how can a gang member have real love for their homie, when they do not have real love for themselves?*

QUOR
J & J
GROCERY·W
BEER·LOTTO
Is this what you want for your life?
OG AVE
LOST Rd
SALE 12·PK CANS 5.99
OPEN
Whats up Fool... what set you from?!

Does Your Gang Have A Retirement Plan?

What benefits will you reap from 20 to 30 years, or even a lifetime of dedicated service invested in your gang? Why is there no retirement plan for gang members? Each and every branch of the military – the Army, Navy, and the Air Force – all have retirement plans as well as their financial benefits in place to show gratitude and appreciation for their sacrifice and/or their years of service. Companies as well as public service workers such as Law Enforcement and Fire Department workers, also have retirement plans in place for their employees. The only thing gang members have to look forward to that remotely resembles retirement is a life time of free room and board and three meals a day in the state penitentiary – all sponsored and paid for by whatever state you happen to reside in. **What benefits will you get for your dedication to your gang?**

WHY IS IT THAT GANG BANGERS FIGHT OVER TURFS, BUT IN THE END, THEY WIND UP SHARING THE SAME YARDS...

the grave yards and prison yards?

What Is To Be Gained Or Won By Gang Wars?

Preparing for war itself is an extremely easy thing to do, but in comparison **with** or **to** preparing for peace, war preparation seems that much easier. Where brains are required to establish and maintain peace, bullets are the only requirements to declare and wage war. Yet, when gangs are presented with a problem, war seems to always be the solution. So ask yourself, *"Why is it that gangs seem to always take the easy way out when it comes to problem solving?" "How much honor should one have being a member of something that always takes the easy way out?"*

Gang members neglect to ask one fundamental question: *"What is there to be gained or won by these wars?"* The majority of wars are fought to gain either: territory, money, oil, or to force one's beliefs upon another.

What is to be gained or won by gang wars? Not oil or not even land is to be won because very few, if any, gangs actually take over their rivals' territory. Gangs seldom, if ever, own any land. So in the event that one does take over their rivals' territory, in all actuality, nothing is really won. Money is definitely not being gained by these wars. We have all heard the popular saying, "Don't go to war unless you got your money right". This is because wars cost money. Guns and bullets cost money. Hospital bills for those injured and lawyer bills for those arrested cost money; not to mention the funeral costs for those who were lost in the wars.

Think about this: One can kill 25 members from a rival set. In the aftermath, instead of your rivals surrendering or bowing down to you or your gang, they will retaliate. Even the weakest gang feels that theirs is the strongest, so they will retaliate to prove this. In that terrible, senseless act where 25 individuals lost their lives, not even respect was gained. *So what, if anything, is being gained – besides filling up the grave yards and prison yards?*

Bangers do not even have to be told what is gained or won from their gang wars. It is sufficient for them to simply seek to win or the desire to

Jeorald Pitts, a.k.a Lil Tone Tone

win even without them knowing what it is that the gang has to win, lose, or gain.

Listen, even if your big homies won't put you up on game, I will. Some of you are fighting in some of the longest wars in American history without a cause or end in sight. Even "Big Tookie Williams", one of the founding fathers of the crips – one of the biggest gangs in the U.S. – admitted in his book, **"Blue Rag, Black Redemption"** that because of immaturity and lack of political leadership, that he and Ramond Washington were never able to develop an agenda or cause for the crips. So in other words, they are rebels without a cause.

Nobody ever wins any gang wars. All that ever happens is that one side loses more than the other. The true meaning of war is not how many battles you fight, but how many you avoid. So, I ask you once again, **"What is being gained or won by gang wars?"**

What Makes You Cool?

Is it because you act a fool? You know it is only one letter that separates the word "cool" from "fool". A lot of people get confused.

What makes you cool? Your tattoos? Being in a gang? The clothes or shoes you sport?

What makes you cool? The jewelry you rock? The way you stroll?

What makes you cool? The people that you hang with? The amount of sex you have had?

What makes you cool? The money in your pocket? The drugs you sell?

If any of these are your definition of cool, then you must have the word confused with fool. Luckily for you, being cool is none of the above, because you cannot **buy** cool or **wear** cool. But, you can **be** cool. Cool is an attitude!!! To have a cool personality is to be laid back, likable, and easy to get along with. Cool is not being hot-headed or angered.

Have you ever heard the saying, "Stay cool, calm, and collected?" A cool person keeps a cool head on his or her shoulders at all times.

R U cool?

Have You Taken
Enough
Time
To
Really
Think
About
Your
Future?
Diploma
J.R.
EASTON
12
9
6
12
3
6

Do You Practice Delayed Gratification?

Delayed gratification is a process of scheduling your work and pleasure in a way that will enhance the pleasure. This can be done by simply postponing your pleasures, and/or focusing on the work at hand; leaving you time and opportunity to fully experience your pleasure, and not having the stresses of knowing there is so much work to be done. It is similar to placing your pleasures in a bank and letting them gain interest so you have more of it later.

Have you ever noticed how the smart kids (nerds) in school really do not have an active social life? Do you recall seeing them being picked on by the popular or so-called "cool kids" simply for trying to get the most out of their education and building their brains?

The whole while the cool kids are not taking their education too seriously, the smart kids are practicing the art of "delayed gratification". They know if they sacrifice the instant gratification of their social life, girlfriends/boyfriends, being popular, etc. while in school and focus on building their brains, later down the line their sacrifices will pay off handsomely. Eventually they will have the best social life and jobs, while also making the good money. They will also have their pick of the most beautiful men and women.

Most of the "cool kids" peak after high school and it is all down hill from there because they were too cool to build their brains in school. They will eventually find themselves working for the "nerds", earning low wages and having to use their hands instead of their heads. They may turn to a life of crime that would most likely land them dead or in jail. Do not be afraid to be smart or a "nerd" because I was a "cool kid" in school, just as most of the men here in prison.

Can you become a forward thinker and practice the art of delayed gratification? Will you pay now and play more later?

What do gang + bang =?

(a) death
(b) prison
(c) pain
(d) All of the above

Is Killing A Rival Worth Spending The Rest Of Your Life In Prison?

Whenever you are out there doing dirt for your hood; set; bario; or turf, if you get caught up (and chances are that you will), with the strict laws that are in place now, you will most likely spend the rest of life in the penitentiary.

The courts are trying young homies as adults from the age of 14. They are handing out life sentences like candy. I am not talking about something I heard, I'm telling you what I see everyday. Young cats are coming in here with it all day. Their faces change, but their frame of mind is always the same – thinking that it was cool to kill their rivals. They fail to realize that when they take a life, they are taking a mother's child, someone's sister or brother, or someone's mother or father.

The cold reality sets in when you come into this small, small world (the penitentiary) with all that time for killing one of your enemies. Then, you will be in here having to kick it with the same enemies and having each others' back under the umbrella of blackness or brownness and so on; because these are the rules. Once you are locked up, most of your homeboys and homegirls will forget about you. Your homeboys are not going to look out for you, your family, or your girlfriend. Well, they may look out for your girl – if you know what I mean.

My point is this – you will be in this hell hole with regret for killing or hurting someone for nothing and doing life for it. Trust me when I tell you this, I see some of the hardest killas from every bario or gang every day, walking these Level 4 yards with forever and a day. They are doing super bad - without money for lawyers, no televisions, or no money to go to the store.

Young homies, you have to ask yourself whether or not you deserve to live life because while you are out there "putting in work", you could be killing yourself in the process. When you are in prison with a life sentence, you are considered "the living dead".

Is laying down a rival's life worth you giving up your own to the pen (penitentiary)?

Do You Believe In You?

If you believe in yourself the way you believe in your hood, you will be successful at anything you choose to do or become – doctor, lawyer, entertainer, athlete, or whatever. The dedication and zeal that you have for banging can be channeled into any of these things and more, but you have to believe that you can become something more than a gang banger. You **must** change that inner picture you have of yourself.

Some of you may think that you are inferior because of where you live, your financial status, or maybe because of your skin color. Regardless of your skin color or financial status, realize that you are inferior to no one. You are descendents of men such as Dr. Martin Luther King, Jr. and Caesar Chavez, just to name a few; strong men with pride and a rich culture behind them that you **can** and **should** be proud of. If only you took the time to learn and explore it yourself, you would be.

You may have excuses ready-made for you of why you think it is destined for you to play the role of gang member, which society has prepared for you - being raised in a single-parent home, living in a gang-infested neighborhood polluted with crime and hopelessness. You can choose to accept this, or you can choose to make your movie more exciting by playing a role that no one expected of you. Look at it this way, life is a big movie and the world is the stage. We are all actors playing roles. Some people choose to play the role of businessmen/women, construction worker, policemen, etc.; while others choose to play the gang banger, drug dealer, or prisoner.

We are playing all of these roles by choice, so you can change your role in life if you really want to. However, you have to prepare by doing certain things first. For example, if you want to play the role of a lawyer, you must first play the role of a law student. If you want to prepare to be a bad boy, then you have to first do bad things. If you want to play the role of prisoner or dead guy in your life's movie, the best way to prepare for those roles is to play the role of a gang banger.

The roles that you play are your choice; some take more preparation than others, but you can play whatever role you want to if you believe in yourself the way you believe in your hood. ***You are the Director and star of your own movie. What role will you play?*** Also be careful of who you have co-starring or guest-starring in your life's movie because their bad acting can ruin it! I hope you win an Academy Award for playing the role of a respectable and highly successful person. ***Can you believe in yourself more than you believe in your gang? What role can you see yourself playing?***

HOW DO YOU THINK YOUR LIFE WOULD BE NOW IF YOU NEVER BANGED?

Are you Really Paying Attention To Your Surroundings?

Just as your body reflects the food you feed it, your mind reflects what its surroundings feed it. ***Have you ever thought about what kind of person you would have been had you been raised in some foreign country? What kinds of food, clothes, entertainment, or sports would you have liked?*** Of course you cannot find the answers to these questions, but chances are that you would not be a gang banger. You would be a different person. ***Why?*** Well, because you would have been influenced by different surroundings. Our environment shapes our beliefs on life and makes us think the way we do.

Try to name a few mannerisms or habits you have that you did not pick up from other people – small things like the way you stroll, stand, or talk; even your choices for music, entertainment, and clothing. It all comes from your surroundings. Too much kickin' it with negative people makes you negative or think negatively. Close contact with petty people develops petty ways in you. On the bright side, hanging with people with big ideas raises your level of thinking. Close contact with ambitious people gives you ambition. Experts say that the person you are today, your personality, ambitions, and present status in life are largely the results of your surroundings. Experts also agree that the person you will become – 1, 2, 10, or 15 years from now – depends a lot on your future surroundings.

Let me put you up on a little game - one of the signs of a negative person is that they usually talk about the past, about how things used to be. Just trip off of it. So choose your homeboys and homegirls wisely. Who you surround yourself with will determine your state of mind more than anything else. Also you will not have to go through the motions of removing the negative people from your life. Just try this experiment. Start changing a few of your negative behaviors to positive ones. For example, if you drink or get high – quit. If you're committing crimes - stop, and so on. Watch and see who will stop kicking it with you.

I personally believe that negative can't stand the sight of positive.

To Bang or Not To Bang: A Book of Questions

WHICH OF YOUR HOMEBOYS/HOMEGIRLS WILL BE AROUND AFTER THE EXPERIMENT?

WILL YOU SURROUND YOURSELF WITH THE RIGHT PEOPLE?

Is There Anything Happening Within Your Gang Now That You Thought Would Never Occur?

From Blacks and Latinos to Asians and Samoans, I've asked hundreds of different gang members this same question and received many responses, but the top three responses were: 1) they didn't think that their gang would have so many different clicks and crews within it like they do now and would be side and street tripping amongst themselves 2) they did not think that their gang, who are supposed to be brothers and sisters – would be turning on each other – displaying jealousy, hate, and killing one another; and the response that is rated number one that I received was 3) they did not think that their gang members would be telling on one another and others as they are doing.

Are any of these three responses on your list of things you did not think would ever go on with or within your gang? Do you think these problems will get better? Gangs have lasted all these years because they have relied on the code of silence. The code has been cracked and the silence has been broken and there is no fixing it, especially with the time the courts are issuing out with their "tough on crime and gang laws". There are reputable gang members and gunners telling on or getting down first, as it is termed these days, and it is only going to get worse; but, as they also say these days, it is what it is. A gang banger would have to be in an awfully bad relationship with reality to think that it makes any kind of sense in today's time to try and build a reputation within his/her gang when it's not even safe to tell your own homeboys/homegirls what you are doing, and a reputation is built on other people knowing what you've done.

I would advise you to reconsider such things before you act. It is no accident that in the U.S. and around the world there is a big increase in the number of people being locked up, especially in America. Just like there is a big increase in telling (snitching). These prisons are filling up from crime partners' testimonies, gang members getting down first to avoid doing time, or to get a reduced sentence. Face the reality. If you are committing crimes and trying to get a rep, you are at a very high risk of insanity and getting ratted on. So, do not act surprised when it happens. As long as there are human beings on the face of the earth, there will be jealousy, favoritism, and separation. These traits really display themselves within a gang setting, so it is no wonder that gangs are clicked and crewed up and often kill one another.

It is hard enough trying to maintain a good relationship with one person, let alone get along with a gang of people; when drugs, guns, liquor, girls, and egos are included. Therefore, it is bound to always be feuds and killings. Have you ever noticed that gang members always seem to separate themselves even if they are from the same gang. For example, some separate themselves by claiming or representing certain sides of the gang – Westside; Eastside; North side; South side; or up, down; front, back; and so on. Then, even if they represent the same side of the gang, to separate themselves again, they represent a certain street or area within that side. Another example – each generation of gang members separates themselves by giving themselves their own title. It just keeps going on and on to the point where you have mini gangs inside of one big gang. Thus, it is not surprising that they are turning on each other.

If you cannot see that with homies from the same set telling on one another and killing each other, that there is no future in gang banging, then what will it take for you to see this? Will it take for you to get told on? Will it take you getting paralyzed? Will it take you having a kid? Will it take you getting a good job? Will it take you going to jail for 1 year, 5 years, or 10 years? Or will it take you having to spend the rest of your life in jail?

What will it take?

Are You Your Own Worst Enemy?

Gang members consider their number one rivals to be their worst enemies due to their attempts to destroy them. However, **have you thought about the idea that you could be more of a threat to your own self than any rival gang, and that you could be your own worst enemy?**

The word self-sabotage, in short, means: the destruction of one's self. Gang bangers have self-destructive habits. They only think about today. They do not concern themselves with the things that they need to preserve their lives. Thus, they are willful agents of their own destruction.

Think about this: you are fortunate enough to live in the land of opportunity – a country where people are fighting to get *into*, instead of fighting to get *out of*; a country where there are fences, not to keep people in, but to keep people from *coming in. How many times have you seen on the news where American citizens are on make-shift rafts trying to escape from this country to a better one?* Despite America's faults, it is still the land of opportunity. *What are you doing with your opportunities? Are you choosing a life of war instead of a life of peace for no good reasons other than for the sake of warring? Doesn't this sound like self-sabotage?*

Wouldn't you say that starving your brain of the knowledge it needs for you to grow is self-sabotage? Wouldn't you say that putting yourself in positions where you know you are going to one day end up in jail is self-sabotage? Wouldn't you say that using drugs, sniffing glue and/or paint is self-destructive? Wouldn't you say that putting yourself in high-risk situations where you could get shot, stabbed, or killed is self-sabotage? Wouldn't you say that by not developing and using your talents that you are blessed with, self-sabotage? If you do not think that it is self-sabotage, then *who is making you do these things? Who is putting the gun to your head?*

Okay. If you are not trying to intentionally sabotage yourself, then *what is stopping you from not doing these things?* It is a fact that it is easier to do what is bad and harmful to one's self than what's beneficial to one's self. ***Do you realize that you are doing more harm to yourself***

than any of your enemies? Just being in a gang is self-destructive, because gangs are the weapons of mass destruction.

After reading this, there may be a war going on inside of you between two desires – self-sabotage versus self-growth – fighting for expression and control. Who wins is up to you. ***Will you continue to be your own worst enemy?***

WHY IS IT SAID THAT THE BEST PLACE TO HIDE SOMETHING FROM A GANG BANGER IS IN A BOOK?

R U Conscious?

What is being conscious?
Consciousness is awareness known or felt by one's inner self, mentally aware or alert. Awareness is the ability to see clearly. What being able to see clearly means is that one must be educated in self and your surroundings. This means that the requirement for consciousness is to have a clear image of one's self and the world in which one finds him/herself.ABus, being conscious is knowing that being a gang banger is not a part of who you are, but a large part of what you do. Being conscious is: knowing that banging is a behavior; and like all learned behavior, it can be unlearned.

Being conscious is: knowing that it is human nature to want to be a part of something, but it is what you choose to be a part of, something productive or something destructive, that makes all the difference in life.

Being conscious is: knowing that a gang banger's dream of a gangsta's paradise of power; riches, and their desire to be number one; and the most feared and respected is an illusion, a mirage to be chased or pursued, but never attained.

Being conscious is: knowing that banging offers a life time of war, a strong likelihood of doing time, and the good chance of being snitched on and dying at an early age.

Being conscious is: knowing the laws and ordinances society has put in place, or putting in place in different cities and states aimed at gang members. For example, in California and other states, there are gang injunctions, "three strikes", and gang enhancement laws where gang members can get up to ten (10) extra years added to their sentences if convicted of any felony, just for being in a gang. There are also probation and parole violations just for being in the presence of another gang member or with anyone else on parole, family included.

Being conscious is: knowing you do not have to allow a life style that you accepted in the past to control your present and your future.

Being conscious is: asking questions and questioning answers.

Being conscious is: knowing that there is little difference between those who ***cannot*** read and those who ***will not*** read.

Jeorald Pitts, a.k.a Lil Tone Tone

Being conscious is: knowing that books hold the information and strategies to the good life and the answers to almost all of life's questions.

Being conscious is: knowing that if you continue doing what you have always done, you will continue getting what you have always gotten.

Being conscious is: knowing if you do not like where you have found your bottom, then change what is going on at the top.

Being conscious is: knowing we are a product of our own thoughts.

Being conscious is: knowing the only limits are the limits established within your own mind.

Being conscious is: knowing what the mind builds in imagination, the mind can build in reality.

Being conscious is: knowing that this consciousness comes at different times for different people.

Being conscious is: knowing that struggle is a fitness routine for your character.

Being conscious is: knowing that good habits are hard to form, but easy to live with; and bad habits are easy to form, but hard to live with.

Being conscious is: knowing what the future holds for you depends on your state of consciousness now.

Being conscious is: knowing there is a difference between an ordinary life and an extraordinary life – and that the difference is simply the word "extra". If you do the extra, you will be extraordinary; but you have to do the extra.

Being conscious is: really knowing you have a light inside of you that is waiting to be turned on so your true character can shine.

Being conscious is: knowing the force that transitions a person from boy to a man, or girl to a woman is consciousness.

R U conscious?

If You Died Today, What Legacy Would You Leave Behind?

The history of the world is simply the stories of what has happened. It is the deeds of a small number of people who decided to use their lives to leave a legacy. Your obituary is a summary of your legacy. I want to ask you a question…***If you died today, what do you think your obituary would say about what you did with your time on earth beyond the standard saying that most obituaries have?*** For example – he/she was a good person; when he/she smiled, they lit up the room; he/she enjoyed spending time with family and friends; and so on.

On the following pages are two obituaries of two very active and reputable gang members who dedicated their whole lives to their gang. Notice how the things that they did for their gang are not mentioned anywhere within either of their obituaries. There is not even mention of their gang names. So think long and hard about this while you are out there turned up and trying to make a name for yourself. It probably will not even be placed in your obituary.

In Loving Memory
of
BYRON A. DANIELS
"TONY"

November 8, 1969 ~ April 20, 1992

Active Pallbearers
KEVIN KONNER
RONALD PYLES
DAMIAN ROBINSON
CHARLES POLK
SHANNON LUCKEY
EUGENE GLOVER

Honorary Pallbearers
Jeorald Pitts - Ramar McMorris - Donald Malone
Avmont Smith - Elbert Taylor - Roderick Barber

To my dearest "Brother" that's so far away, I'd give anything to have you for one more day.

To tell you something you already knew, that I'll miss you and I needed you and I love you.

I know in my heart that you are at peace, but the pain it won't stop, it just won't cease.

It seems like yesterday we were fussing and fighting, now all I find myself doing is hurting and crying

Right now I know it seems like a heavy load, but my tears will dry up cause I'll see you again, I'll see you at the crossroads.

Love You Forever and
Forever In My Memory
SIS

IN LOVING MEMORY

Iwori Wotura Odom

MAY 6, 1972 ~ APRIL 5, 2003

The Lord is my shepherd: I shall not want. He maketh me to lie down in green pastures: he leadeth me beside the still waters.
He restoreth my soul: he leadeth me in the paths of righteousness for his name's sake.
Yea, though I walk through the valley of death, I will fear no evil: for thou art with me; thy rod and thy staff they comfort me.
Thou preparest a table before me in the presence of mine enemies: thou anointest my head with oil; my cup runneth over. Surely, goodness and mercy shall follow me all the days of my life: and I will dwell in the house of the Lord forever.

23rd Psalm

Proceeding Iwori in Death:
Father, Kenneth Odom
Mother, Gloria Jean Davis
Grandmother, Cora Mae Davis

Iwori leaves to cherish him in memory
Xenia Odom, Akia Odom, Jailah Johnson, (Daughters)
William Davis (Grandfather), William Davis Jr. (Uncle)
Iva Jackson, Joyce E. Davis, LeeScherry Davis, (Aunts)
Anthony Lee, Mr. & Mrs. La'Shaun D. Davis,
Cora Jean Barnett, Billy Davis, Malissia Davis, (1st Cousins)
Broadrick Davis, Samuel Bryant, Shaunte Rene Davis, Da'Shaun Davis,
Kieara Lee, Kashayla Lee, (2nd Cousins)
And of course his extended family and friends.

Iwori you will be truly missed... so in your memory we will make each day a magnificent adventure. Accept the challenges that may come our way. Seize each opportunity that we find without concern for what others might say. Experience each day with open arms, savoring both victory and strife, welcoming the good and the bad together. For only then will we know the joy of life.

Jeorald Pitts, a.k.a Lil Tone Tone

What I'm trying to put you up on is that the things that make you most proud as a gang member do not even make your obituary. Trust that it will not express how he/she was a turned-up rider; how he/she fought, stabbed, and/or shot x-amount of enemies; or how he/she did x-amount of time in jail, stayed down and never snitched on anyone.

Think about this: you are dedicating your life to something that your family will not see fit to put in your obituary. It will not count in the end. ***Do you want your legacy to mean more and last longer than the spray paint on the walls with R.I.P after your name?***

What Legacy Would You Like To Leave?

Do you want to be able to leave your footprints in the sands of time so future generations will know and benefit from what you did while you were here on this earth?

Now that you have thought about what you think your obituary would say, if you died today, I ask that you do this exercise: Ask yourself what legacy you want to leave when you *do* finally depart from this earth. Then write down what you think your obituary is going to say about what you would have accomplished in your lifetime.

Here are a few ideas to help you get your thoughts flowing; but only you know what you want your legacy to be, these are only examples.

He/She was a great parent and raised _____ successful children.

He/She was a mentor to _____.

He/She was a community leader.

He/She fought hard for _____.

He/She owned and operated a successful business of _____.

He/She acquired a degree in _____.

He/She played in the _____.

He/She invented _____.

Do this exercise at this time

Now that you have completed this exercise you should have a better idea of how you want to be remembered. It is time to make it do what it

Jeorald Pitts, a.k.a Lil Tone Tone

do. You have to take charge of your life and accomplish your goals and dreams. It is very important that you maintain a positive outlook on life that says "yes, I can". If you think you can, you can! Though, of course, the opposite is also true. If you think you can't, you are also correct. It is your choice. What you do today will decide your legacy tomorrow.

What will your legacy be?

Lil Tone with his homies on the Maximum Security Yard at Lancaster Prison '94.

Folsom Prison '96.

Lil Tone at Salinas Valley State Prison '97.

Lil Tone's homeboy, Pete, posing for a picture in a federal prison just a few years after getting the murder charges dismissed against him that Lil Tone was found guilty of. Pete is now serving a 22-year-sentence for drug trafficking.

Lil Tone at age 28 in Lancaster Prison Visiting Room

Quest For Answers

This morning as I am walking through the corridor on my way to the exercise yard, the bright signs posted everywhere warning that there are no warning shots seems to be popping out at me in 3-D today. Upon reaching the door, the sun rays appeared then disappeared as if the sun was playing hide and seek with the clouds. As I surveyed my surroundings, the cold frigid air hit against my face, but still I was burning hot. I got word the night before that my OG homeboy had a fight with a dude from another gang and had come out on the losing end. I noticed that there were two groups huddled up like two opposing football teams. Now, you would think these cats would be spending their time trying to find a way out of prison, rather than planning and preparing for battle. As I was strolling over to my team, I could recognize the silent cheers through slight gestures such as head nods or thumbs up from the fans in their state blues waiting to see who was going to win. My OG homeboy - who is only 5'5" and 150 pounds soaking wet with rocks in his pockets – was in the middle of the huddle like a quarterback, giving a play-by-play on what went down the night before. As I approached, I noticed that he had what appeared to be black protection paint around his eyes like football and baseball players wear. Upon further review, I realized that his eyes were indeed black, but not from any type of paint. He was explaining how the incident was over a debt for two caps of weed, valued at $20. When it became impossible for me to listen any further (staring at his big black eyes), I lost all reasoning and understanding as violent thoughts ran rampant through my mind; leaving room for no other thoughts to enter. Just as my team was setting up a play to "bum rush" their whole crew, my reasoning returned like a throwback jersey. I spoke up and said, "I'll handle it myself". Although my reasoning had returned, understanding was nowhere to be found within me. I strolled over to their huddle requesting to talk to their shot-caller, a dude I knew to be trained in martial arts. At that moment, this was of no concern to me. I had my "are you ready to rumble" theme music playing loud in my head and the look of revenge and destruction plastered on my face. Now face-to-face with their shot-caller, I could read the concern in one of his eyes, and readiness revealed in the other. I told him that in order to prevent a war I had to have a head-up fade with the guy responsible for painting my homeboy's eyes. He went back to his huddle and relayed my request, only to return a minute later to let me know the dude did not want to fight me because my homeboy was the one in the wrong and furthermore, he knew that I was skilled with my hands and feet from seeing me in action many times before. Thus, my fight request was not granted. His team was protecting him from what my team and I felt he had coming. See, in here, when someone puts hands on one of yours – whether they are in the right or wrong – you have to retaliate. Yes, I did say right *or* wrong. So we blitzed their whole team and a riot broke out with no referee to blow a whistle and stop the play. The only sounds you heard were gunshots from a Mini-14 Rifle being fired by the guards in the several gun towers surrounding the yard. We were in the center of the yard covered by a cloud of dust, just like in the cartoons, created by all of the dirt we were kicking up as we got crackin'. Over 20 rounds were fired and I could hear the bullets whizzing past my head. At the rate that I was dodging bullets; fists; and knives, I was beginning to feel like Neo from The Matrix.

When the dust cleared, one person was shot in the chest, two left unconscious, two guys stabbed, one broken jaw, and a lot of bruised egos. All 32 of us who were involved were arrested and taken to jail inside of jail – The Hole. In the hole, you lose what little freedoms you do have while in prison, starting with not being able to use the phone. Then, there are the visits- where you may have enjoyed 5 hours of quality time with your loved ones and receiving that much-needed hug and kiss; that is all over with. You are only allowed 1 hour and no hugs or kisses, because you are separated by a Plexiglas partition and have to talk through a speaker or phone. You are only allowed out of your cell for 10 hours a week to go to a small cage that resembles a dog kennel. The process you go through just to get to the kennel is so degrading. You have to strip all of your clothing off while another man looks you over. The whole while, your cellie is less than 6 feet behind you. Then, you have to squat and cough three times. You repeat this process upon your return from the cage as well. I have gotten naked for more prison guards than I have for women. I can go on forever telling you how bad the hole is, but I am going to get back to the story. Trust me when I tell you, it is a place you would rather read about than experience the reality of. Prison period, is way worse than anything you see on TV. The next day after the uproar, while sitting in the hole - our bodies and eyes still burning from the strong pepper spray that was used to

Jeorald Pitts, a.k.a Lil Tone Tone

try and stop the rumble – my cellie and I were talking about the incident and asking ourselves how we would feel if the homeboy who had gotten shot in the chest died for backing another homie who was in the wrong by not paying a $20 debt. We were also wondering who, if anyone, really won this battle considering the fact that we all ended up in the hole facing an additional year, which would be added to our sentences for participation in a riot. In here, who started what does not matter. Participate, and you are guilty. While these questions were searching for answers in our minds, I heard the rattle of an officer's keys as he was walking down the tier passing out love via mail. As the rattle became louder and as he approached my cell, I was sure that he would zoom past because normally, you do not receive mail the next day after coming to the hole. Yet, he stops in front of our cell and says, "Pitts!" With a country drawl and grinning, he says, "I got two pieces of mail for you" There was something puzzling in his grin – the way the corners of his mouth were raised. This, he presented as a smile with both of his eyebrows standing at attention over his eyes; that held a strange glance. I coolly bounced to the door with the swagger of a badger, matching his stare with one of disregard of my own; slightly surprised, however, because mail in here has a strange way of disappearing into the dark corners of this place when you get into trouble. He handed me the mail with his lazy grin, his teeth displaying his dislike for toothbrushes. As he stands at the door waiting on me to open my mail, I dismissed him with a jerk of my thumb and rushed to open the first piece of mail. It was a letter from my sister along with an obituary. I just knew that it would be one of my homeboys on it before I even pulled it out of the envelope. My heart dropped to my stomach as I pulled it from the envelope and my assumption was confirmed. I quickly skimmed through the letter to see what gang was responsible for his demise. My heart was racing like a NASCAR as I seemed to go straight to the part of who did it and how. The answer hit me like a Mike Tyson right hook. It was the gang from which my cell mate was a member of; the same person who just 24 hours ago, had my back, risking his life right alongside of me in the riot. A host of conflicting emotions came over me and my first reaction to such a devastating blow was to kick and punch the door. See, in here, our gangs (me and my cellie's) kick it and ride together. However, on the streets, they are #1 enemies and constantly killing each other.

This situation really confused me, and my confusion was turned into anger as I tore into the next piece of mail. It was an envelope with a return address of a California Ku Klux Klan office. I opened the letter and the

To Bang or Not To Bang: A Book of Questions

first thing that caught my eye was the big congratulations typed in bold print at the top of the letter – **CONGRATULATIONS**. The KKK was congratulating me for my work as a gang member. It further thanked me for continuing their work and making it so that they did not have to work so hard anymore. Take note of how he thanked me for making it so they did not have to work so hard – they did not say retire, letting it be known that they were still at work. This letter went on to say that they now know that all Blacks are not lazy, because crips and bloods work 24 hours a day trying to kill each other, selling drugs to their own people and committing crimes. Then the letter read in bold print that the crips and bloods invented something to destroy Blacks even better than any plan the Klan could have ever envisioned. The crips and bloods allow them to kill two birds with one stone. One kills the other, while the killer goes to their new and improved plantation – prison. Lastly, the letter stated that the Klan wanted to thank me for my life time pledge to bang. This letter from the Klan and the obituary arriving at the same time was no coincidence. It was at this point that I understood why I got my mail so quickly and why this pale-faced officer smiled at me the way he did. They wanted to humiliate me. See, the officers read our mail and they knew that my letter contained an obituary of one of my homeboys recently killed due to gang violence. They also knew what the KKK stated in their letter. However, the letter and obituary arriving at the same time hit me with a double barrel of reality and anger. My eyes started to sting with the threat of unknown tears. I begged them silently not to betray me in front of my cellie. I had a reputation to maintain; but my tears, being as rebellious as I was, flowed unchecked down my cheeks, off my chin, and onto the letter. Years of stored-up tears were released from all that time when I thought that not only was crying a sign of sadness, but also a sign of weakness. But these tears were different. They seemed to bring with them a sense of clarity and strength, and when they dried up, a rainbow of questions came over me; for instance, *am I really doing the KKK's job? How can gangs be allies in jail and #1 adversaries on the streets?* And, *why haven't I questioned my banging belief to see if they really make sense?* For the next couple of months, these questions along with the questions my father would regularly pose to me would keep popping up in my mind. The search for the answers to all of these nagging questions would start me on my quest for answers through deep self-reflection and studying. To keep it real, I did not really want to find anything that would break my long-held belief of banging that was rapped in layers of dedication and sacrifice. In fact, I was

Jeorald Pitts, a.k.a Lil Tone Tone

hoping to find answers that would support my belief and silence all of the questions. Just the thought of what I have been representing and putting my life on the line for, not being what I believed it to be was scary.

However, the more I engaged in studying, self-reflection, and questioning; the more I learned about myself and the framework of gangs. I even wrote the co-founder of the crips, Stanley "Tookie" Williams (May he rest in peace), on death row and questioned him. I learned that while forming the crips, the gang had no agenda, goals, or cause behind it other than the destruction of other black gangs; which really could be seen as doing the job of the Ku Klux Klan.

I read the Mexican Mafia gang member – Art Blojas' – book, **Blood In Blood Out**; which gave me his very insightful views on gangs and the reason as to why he left his gang after sacrificing so much to be a part of it; I also read Naim Akbar's, **Community of Self**; which gave me a good description of manhood; Dennis P. Kimbro's, **What Makes the Great, Great** was another book I read - a book that breaks down the character traits of great people of both the past and the present; I studied James Allen's, **As a Man Thinketh**; which taught me about the power of positive thoughts.

All of this new-found knowledge was opening my eyes to the many flaws, cracks, and holes in the foundation of the gang life style to the point that I was starting to feel uncomfortable even having my love and loyalty placed upon it.

I began to regularly examine my thoughts and actions after reading the book *7 Habits of Highly Effective People* by Stephen R. Covey. It was through this book that I learned that we are creatures of habit and we sometimes believe in ideas and do things that are not good for us or no longer even make sense to us solely out of habit. *7 Habits* helped me realize why it was so hard for me to replace my wrong actions and beliefs with the right ones that I was discovering. I cannot say exactly when my change in thinking really kicked in. It was not like something really bad happened that rocked my faith in banging. I had been shot several times and received a life sentence and *that* hadn't rocked my belief. It had more to do with the little feelings deep inside that we all were born with of right and wrong; that many of us suppress – some better than others. These feelings were feeding on all of the questions I was asking myself. The feelings of right were getting bigger and stronger and started to attack my wrong beliefs. There were small wars going on inside of my mind and heart.

My gang beliefs that held dominance for over 20 years, was losing ground. The feeling of right started to take control. I had to admit to myself that I had been mislead into believing that banging was cool and had a cause behind it. As a result, my life had been filled with misconceptions, mischief, misconduct, and mistrust; all from this one misjudgment. This further fueled my passion for knowledge.

My conduct became different from most prisoners, especially gang members. I acquired an extreme desire for knowledge, looting the prison library and having all of my family and friends to order books for me to quench my new-found thirst for the written word. I did not read many novels because, for me, reading was not an escape from reality; but to enhance the reality in which I lived. I found comfort in books in this uncomfortable place - reading over 750 books - thus, turning the state pen into my own Penn State.

I secretly starting talking to and questioning other gang members, here in prison, of many different races. I found that a lot of them felt that they wasted their lives gang banging and if they had a chance to do it all over again that they would not choose this life style. Yet and still, they held onto this self-destructive way of living because it was all they knew. They lacked the strength to venture off into the unknown and stand alone. A big part of the unknown was what might happen if one tried to leave their gang.

In prison, leaving your gang by any other means than going to God or going into protective custody is very risky and is considered unacceptable. For someone to just quit because they came to realize that the gang life no longer made any sense to them might be taken as a slap in the face to those who are putting their lives on the line every day for their gangs. Nothing else makes sense to them other than their gang beliefs. Those who might try to leave their gang, their deaths could serve as an example for anyone else who might be tempted to try and leave, so I held my views to myself until the time was right. My homeboys started slowly noticing changes in me and not just because I was studying a lot. The decisions that I was making within the gang were based more on intelligence and common sense, rather than violence first – as in the past.

I decided to confide in another ranking member and ask for his support in my leaving the gang on the terms that I no longer believe in it wholeheartedly. I explained to him that I could not continue to do it half-heartedly because I would be doing a disservice to the gang and to myself. After an hour of us talking and of me enlightening him on my new outlook on life, he saw my passion and courage and decided to support my walking away from

Jeorald Pitts, a.k.a Lil Tone Tone

the gang. However, I still had to take it to the gang as a whole. Securing his support was a big step, but I knew beforehand that I had a very good chance of obtaining his support because he would move up into my position when I left and I would endorse him as a worthy replacement.

I called a meeting for the next day to announce my departure. That night I rehearsed what I was going to say as if I was going on trial; which in a way I would be, because they could oppose my leaving and try to inflict bodily harm upon me, so as to not appear weak to the other gangs or keep the door closed that I would open up if I was allowed to walk away unharmed.

First hope rolled into my mind as I was really excited about the possibilities of becoming a man for the first time and not a member; but then it was followed by dreadful numbing fear. This fear sparked many questions. *What would my fellow members think of me? How will they react? Will they force me to do something to them? Or, will they try to do something to me? Would they still respect me?*

I knew I would be disappointing many of them who really looked up to me because the flames from my fire for banging burned brightly in this dark place. I would be armed, but I knew at least five of them would be armed as well. It was a rule that I had put in place that at least five people be armed at all times while on the yard.

The questions of what might happen to me and what my homeboys, home girls, and others would think of me kept running through my mind. However, I began replacing them with more empowering questions, like *– What would happen to me if I did not leave? What would I think of myself if I continued to stand for something I no longer believed in or that no longer made any sense to me?* These are the questions that I allowed to dwell in my mind, not the ones produced by fear. Through my studies, I learned that fear is an emotion that prevents us from taking action and making change. Fear comes from not knowing if the action we want to take is the best one. It is how we handle fear and the questions fear produces that make the difference in our lives. The next day, despite the fear displayed by the tornado of butterflies twisting around in my stomach, I proceeded to the meeting.

Upon arriving at the area of the yard we kicked it in, I noticed the curiousness on the faces of all my homies to learn the reason for this meeting. I quickly called the meeting to order and was encased in a circle of about 35 members. I first reminded them of some of the sacrifices I had made to be in a position of influence. Then I told them "I was stepping back from

To Bang or Not To Bang: A Book of Questions

the gang to try and change my life for the better, and I know some of you may not understand or even like my decision; but I am just as serious about my changing as I was about my banging. So, it is not because I have lost my heart, it is because I found myself." I further said to them, "I know the unwritten rule about my decision to leave; however, I hope the respect you have for me as a member will carry over to you respecting my choice to become a grown man for the first time in my life. I will not insult you with all of my reasons as to why I have decided to stand alone. It has nothing to do with any of you, but everything to do with me. I will just say that I have come across some very important information that compelled me to go in this direction. This life style is no longer compatible with my personal standards, goals, and new way of thinking." I said, "I am leaving at the top without any scandal or smut. I just want to focus on my own life for a change and I ask that you brothas do not try and stand in my way. I will not be running to religion or a protective custody yard to walk away ***from*** something that I gave so many years of sacrifice and dedicated service ***to***."

After my speech, everyone had very surprising expressions on their faces. My announcement caught them off guard. I thought I would be attacked at any moment, then one of my homies that I had mentored stared at me with a real puzzling look. His left eye was wide open, but his right eye more hooded. He asked me with a voice of disappointment, "Are you doing this because you really no longer want to be a part of this, or are you doing it to try to make a play to get out of prison?" I responded, "I was for real, and I am doing it because I do not believe in what banging is all about anymore." Then I made my way out of the crowd. I knew if I was able to walk out of that circle that I stood a good chance of walking away from the gang without any harm. After walking out of the crowd, I was still unsure of how they would react, but they knew I was prepared to die for my new-found beliefs. They remained in a huddle formation, discussing my decision like a jury in deliberation, for about 30 minutes. To me though, it seemed like forever due to my nervousness. The verdict was in – I would not be opposed.

I later learned that some of them even envied me for being man enough to stand up for my beliefs of wanting to stand alone; which takes more courage than being from a gang, where you have a gang of people standing with you.

I was free! This freedom was giving me the chance to view life through the lenses of Mr. Pitts, grown ass man; instead of through the lenses of Lil Tone, gang member. I really liked the colorful possibilities that I was

Jeorald Pitts, a.k.a Lil Tone Tone

seeing. It was as if my banging perspective had me viewing life in black and white, and now I was seeing life in high definition color.

I was now free from the invisible chains of gang customs, which are more binding than any handcuffs or barbed wire fences. I was excited to be able to tell someone I was my own man. When they asked me *"what set you from?"* I would no longer be living by the second-hand, hand-me-down, street codes, or ideas of what it takes to be real; handed down by the OGs who came before me. Those things only led to the three Ps – pain, prison, and pushin' up daisies. These street codes and customs had me trading in my self-respect and principles for street and prison respect for years. This had gotten to the point where I had a lot of street and prison respect, but lacked self-respect; which caused me to make so many self-destructive decisions.

My first step was to gain my self-respect through self-education and build my character and reputation as a man instead of a member. I constructed my own codes and philosophies. I took my destiny into my own hands based on my first-hand experiences. Although I could not go back and make a brand new start, I could start from now and make a brand new ending.

Mr. Pitts with his daughter, Shenikwa; and his sister, Cherise.

Mr. Pitts getting some love from his family on a visit.

Mr. Pitts with his father, Mr. Sabra Pitts (R.I.P), in the visiting room.

Mr. Pitts packing a new kind of weapon.

Afterthoughts

Maybe in the past, so-called experts have hit you with their drive-by journalist views of gang life. I, for one, do not believe that anyone from outside the madness of inner city gang life can fully understand it. This is why I have highlighted my life experiences, lessons learned, and questions to enlighten you - as I have bottled up every tear drop that I have ever shed from the lost lives due to gang violence, all of the pain that this life style has ever brought upon me, and sprinkled it throughout these writings. I hope you have picked up what I have put down because it is real; as my heart, mind, and body still bares the scars of these ordeals and events. **Will you allow my tribulations to help you to experience a better life?**

If I can stop banging in this dream graveyard (prison), I know you can do it wherever you may be. You just have to **decide** to do it, and **do** it. I believe that as humans, in the deepest parts of ourselves, that we all want to do something positive and go beyond ourselves. It is not where we start out that matters, but the questions we ask ourselves and the decisions we make about where we are determined to end up that really matter.

The questions you ask yourself determine how you think, what you focus on, how you feel, and what you do. Successful people ask better questions, so they tend to receive better answers – answers that let them know what to do to get the best results. For example, a good question would be: **What can I do to help myself stop banging?** A good question asks your mind for answers and solutions. A bad question would be: **Why can't I stop banging?** The bad question is asking your mind for excuses.

The following exercise is the final series of questions in this book. However, I would ask that you write your answers down in as much detail as possible. The purpose of writing your answers down helps in the process of thinking and also will afford you the opportunity to go back and re-read them at a later date.

1. *Why do you bang?*

2. *What is the cause, goal, or aim of your gang?*

3. *If you would have grown up in your rival's territory do you think you would have been from your rival gang?*

4. *If you could change one thing about gang banging what would you change?*

5. *If you really put your mind to becoming something other then a gang banger, what would you become?*

6. *What would you have to change in your life in order to accomplish this?*

7. *Do you have the courage and heart to stop banging?*

8. *Will you stop banging? And why?*

9. *What have you learned from reading this book?*

Some of the questions throughout this book may not seem to have an immediate value or you may have yet to find your answers to, but you will remember them vividly, and wonder about them until some later experience helps give you the answers and their meaning.

I would like to thank you for allowing me the opportunity to pose these questions to you as I find small pieces of freedom in doing so. Also, it allows me to restore my sense of meaning and responsibility to myself, to you, and to society. Do not get me wrong, I am not a moral warrior. I have my faults; however, my moral compass is pointing towards lacing you with the real as a way of righting some of my wrongs.

Jeorald Pitts, a.k.a Lil Tone Tone

If you have any questions that you would like to ask me or just want to write to let me know how this book affected you, please do. I would like to hear from you…

I can be reached via e-mail at:

jp2bangornot2bang@yahoo.com

Or

By writing to:

Level 4 Publishing
1840 S. Gaffey Street
Suite #248
San Pedro, CA 90731

For book order go to:
tobangornottobang.com

I was 17 years old when my journey started. I was busted for a car-jacking with firearm, along with "gang enhancements". The judge gave me 17 years and 4 months (that was 7 years and 4 months for the car-jacking **and** the gun, and 10 years for gang enhancement). That was longer than I had been here on this earth! I received more time for being a gang member than I received for the "car-jacking" and "gun".

When I hit prison, it was like the land of the lost! There are lots of rules that you <u>have</u> to follow; more-so when you are a homie/southern. When rules are broken, it could cost you your life! Me, I'm tattooed from head to toe. Being young and banged out, I wanted everybody and their mommas to know where I was from and how much I truly loved my hood – also that I was super hard! Some people take my tats as a sign of aggression; so sometimes, people do not know how to get at you right.

I ended up with a drug debt that was not mine. I got into it and went heads up with another homie for $150. He had a knife and I did not – thinking that I was "Billy Bad Ass". I almost lost my life. Prison life is not a joke, so please think about it and take this story seriously.

The author of this book asked me some questions that made me seriously think about my life, and shot me some books to read that helped open my young eyes. I am only 22 years old, the author gave me some game, and he made me see my life is worth something. I am truly thankful to him and forever in his debt. I am happy to report that I have been off of any and all drugs and have been working hard on building myself to be a better person inside and out; not only for myself, but for my family and loved ones!

----------------------------------TRUE STORY----------------------------
FRANK ERIK RODRIGUEZ aka BOY BLUE
V*NORWALK

2009
Kern Valley State Prison

It Took 45 To Life...
Don't Let It Happen To You

Right now I am sitting in a 5x8 cell because I didn't listen when I was young. So, if you give me a moment of your time, I'll show you why you should listen.

When I was young, I would see all of my other cousins and their friends gang bangin' like it was the thing to do, so to me, it was the coolest thing in the world. I would tell myself that one day, I am going to bang. No one could tell me nothing. I knew what I wanted to be – a full-time banger.

I started trying to bang at a young age; and in the end, I had my life taken away from me at a young age as well. I was only 16 years old when I got sentenced to 45 years to life for a crime that I did not commit, or even know about. I am sitting in prison with life just for being in a gang.

You may ask yourself, how can somebody get all of that time for being in a gang. All they need is for somebody to say that you did something because gang members are number one suspects. You may think that this cannot happen to you. I know this, because I used to think the same way; but I have news for you – it can happen to any gang member. At the time of me getting life, I was housed in Juvenile Hall and as I sat there with all of this time, I never even got so much as a licked stamp from any of my so-called homies. So, I told myself that I am going to put my life in check – as a man, not as a banger. I sat in that small cell lost in my thoughts and my misery. As I was doing this, I was seeing so many gang members come and go and I couldn't help but ask myself, **will I ever be free again? Will I ever get the chance to do something right with my life and make something out of myself?** When I started asking myself these questions and really wanting to make something out of myself, I thought it was too late because I had 45 to life – not for something I did, but for something that I didn't do.

So I found a way out, by the means of a "break-out". I broke out of the halls at the age of 17 and I stayed on the run for more than 3½ years.

In those 3½ years, I had 2 kids – a boy and a girl – that I love with all my heart and would do anything for. But there is one thing that I may never get the chance to do, and that's see my babies grow up, or tuck them in the bed before they go to sleep, or protect them like a father should; because I could only run from my past for so long, and now my kids have to suffer because of my past as a gang member.

In this short life of mine, I have lost a lot and I have grown tired of losing and seeing my young people losing because they want to be a gang banger. I only wish that I had what you have and that is the chance to be free and be with my family.

Trust me, what you are trying **to do**, has already **been done**, and the result is failure; because you can never accomplish anything good by bangin'.

I hope what I have told you about my life as a banger has woke something up in you and made you start thinking about your life. I once heard someone say that bangin' is not a life style, but a death style.

So, I say to you…

…to bang or not to bang…the choice is yours.

KENNETH GILLIAM a.k.a FOOTS
ROLLIN' 60s

Why?

- *Why are we drawn to those things that destroy us?*
- *Why do our lives seem to be driven by greed and lust?*
- *Why do we belittle our humanity by the lives that we take?*
- *Why do we continuously disrespect ourselves by the choices that we make?*
- *Why is our nation drowning in blindness?*
- *Why don't we show ourselves love & kindness?*
- *Why don't we make it possible for our people to see peaceful days?*
- *Why has our vision become blurred to the point of being hazed?*
- *Why does it seem like we hate ourselves?*
- *Why do we continue to live in a state of existence equal to hell?*
- *Why don't we care about our tomorrows?*
- *Why don't we leave a legacy of progress for our people to follow?*
- *Why don't we gain knowledge and open our eyes?*
- *Why do we act like we are afraid to rise?*
- *Why?*

Written by: JERMAINE SMOTHERS